Smoothies
And Shakes

Also Includes Smoothie Mixes!

Jackie Gannaway

COPYRIGHT © 2005

All rights reserved. Written permission must be secured
from the publisher to use or reproduce any part of this book.
Permission is granted for brief quotations in critical reviews or articles.

Published in Austin, TX by COOKBOOK CUPBOARD
P.O. Box 50053, Austin, TX 78763
(512) 477-7070 phone   (512) 891-0094 fax
ISBN 1-885597-54-1

NOTICE: The information contained in this book is true, complete, and accurate to the best of my knowledge. All recommendations and suggestions are made without any guaranty on the part of the editor or Cookbook Cupboard. The editor and publisher disclaim any liability incurred in connection with the use of this information.

Artwork by Frank Bielec of Mosey 'N Me - Katy, TX

Over 2 1/2 Million Copies Of Jackie Gannaway's Books Are In Print!

ORDER OUR 40 BOOK TITLES FROM
CookbookCupboard.Com

Mail Order Information

To order a copy of this book send a check for $3.95 + $1.50 for shipping (TX residents add 8.25 % sales tax) to Cookbook Cupboard, P.O. Box 50053, Austin, TX 78763. Send a note asking for this title by name.

Another book you might enjoy is "Cupshakes" - mixes for drinks, puddings and ice cream to be shaken up in a paper cup with a lid.

If you like the recipe for "Milk Shakers" on Pg. 32 of this book, you might want to order "Special Spoonfuls". It has mixes in spoons for hot or cold drinks, dips, dessert cheeseballs and more. There is only one shipping charge per order.

If you would like a descriptive list of the 40 fun titles in The Kitchen Crafts Collection, send a note, call, or fax asking for a brochure.
Phone 512 477-7070   Fax 512 891-0094

Smoothies And Shakes

This book features recipes for fruit smoothies, non-fruit smoothies, milkshakes, malts, blender cocktails and even mixes for smoothies.

The cocktails are "fancy" creamy drinks made by adding liquor to a rich shake or smoothie. The rich shakes and smoothies really can be served as dessert with or without the alcohol. There is one mix in a spoon for "Milk Shakers" on Pg. 32. Give that a try with kids for a fun little project.

Mixes And Sugar Free Mixes

Mixes for smoothies and frozen cappuccinos are included. These mixes can be made sugar free if desired. Keep the mixes on hand for a fast smoothie for yourself or give them as part of a gift basket or hostess gift.

These basic mix recipes can be made in limitless flavors. (Pgs.4-8). If you plan to make mixes in quantity buy the ingredients at places like Sam's Club or Costco for economy.

Ingredients

Fruit smoothies are very versatile. Use any kind of 100% juice or a juice blend (some juice blends are 100% juice and others contain added sugar and are not 100% juice - read the label).

Use frozen fruit in smoothies to help thicken and chill the smoothie. You don't need any ice when using frozen fruit. Buy frozen fruit in bags in the freezer case or cut up fruit and freeze it to use in smoothies.

Plain or flavored yogurt can be added to any fruit smoothie - use flavor suggested in the recipe or use any flavor you want. Same with sherbet, ice cream, sorbet - use any flavor - use sugar free or light ice cream if desired.

Substituting Ingredients

Substitute any fruits or juices in the fruit smoothie recipes. If a recipe calls for "1 cup orange juice" - feel free to change that to a different juice or to use two juices - make that "1/2 cup orange juice and 1/2 cup strawberry nectar", if that is what you have on hand or want to try.

Change the fruits to any you want. Remember fruits work best if frozen.

What if I don't need a blender full?

You can easily cut these recipes in half, but I would make a whole recipe in order to have leftovers. Freeze leftover smoothies either in one dish (and eat like ice cream) or freeze into ice cubes (and put in a glass with Sprite or 7-Up as a drink - or - whirl the smoothie ice cubes in a blender with Sprite or 7-Up or with milk or juice to make another smoothie). Put one or two frozen smoothie ice cubes into a champagne glass and top with champagne.

Smoothies For Breakfast?

Add 1/2 cup of granola to any fruit smoothie.

Blender

In order for the blender to do the work for you it needs to be able to crush ice. I used cubes from my ice maker and that worked fine. Or use bagged crushed ice. Large size ice cubes won't work - most blenders can't crush large ice cubes efficiently.

Adding Supplements To Smoothies

Talk to your doctor before adding any supplements (available at health food stores) to smoothies. You want to be sure the supplements will really help you and not have any harmful effect. You also need medical advice on the amount to add and how much per day is advisable.

Jackie Gannaway

Mix For Frozen Cappuccino
(Make limitless flavors - see Pg. 8)

1/2 cup powdered coffee creamer - Choose any flavor - see flavor list on Pg. 8.
1/4 cup General Foods International Coffees® - Choose any flavor - see flavor list on Pg. 8.
1 Tb. instant coffee powder (or granules, or crystals)
1/4 cup powdered sugar
Opt: 1 tsp. cinnamon
Opt: 2 Tb. Nesquik® or similar chocolate drink powder
   (Add this for mocha flavor.)

1. Mix all dry ingredients in a small bowl.
2. Place mix into a zipper sandwich bag.
3. Decorate if giving as a gift (see Pg. 5)
4. Attach instructions below.

Frozen Cappuccino
Make a blender full of Frozen Cappuccino with this mix!

1. Place 2 cups milk (or water) into a blender.
2. Add mix and blend briefly.
3. Add 3 cups crushed ice (or small cubes) and blend until smooth and creamy.
4. Add 1 cup vanilla or coffee flavored ice cream if desired and blend until smooth.

Makes approx. 4 cups.

How To Serve Frozen Cappuccino At Home
(Instead of making a mix.)

   This is a great drink to make for yourself and company. Do it this way:
   Start with your blender and the instructions in the box above. Place milk in blender. Then add the ingredients that go into the mix directly into the blender - (powdered coffee creamer, etc.)
   Blend briefly. Add ice and blend well. Add ice cream if desired. You will have a blender full of Frozen Cappuccino to enjoy.

Give This Frozen Cappuccino Mix As A Gift
   Read about this on Pg. 5.

Mix For Sugar Free Frozen Cappuccino

1/2 cup powdered coffee creamer, unflavored
1/4 cup General Foods International Coffees® - Cafe Vienna, French Vanilla Cafe or Suisse Mocha all come in a sugar free version. All of these flavors work well in this recipe.
1 Tb. instant coffee powder (or granules, or crystals)
1/3 cup Splenda® sugar substitute
Opt: 1 tsp. cinnamon
Opt: 2 Tb. sugar free Nesquik® chocolate drink powder for a mocha flavor.

1. Mix all dry ingredients in a small bowl.
2. Place mix into a zipper sandwich bag.
3. Decorate if giving as a gift (see Pg. 5).
4. Attach instructions below.

Sugar Free Frozen Cappuccino
Make a blender full of Iced Cappuccino with this mix!

1. Place 2 cups milk (or water) into a blender.
2. Add mix and blend briefly.
3. Add 3 cups crushed ice (or small cubes) and blend until smooth and creamy.

Makes approx. 4 cups.

How To Serve Sugar Free Frozen Cappuccino At Home (instead of making a mix)

Read about this on Pg. 4. Follow those instructions with this recipe.

Give This Frozen Cappuccino Mix As A Gift

This is easy to give as a gift. With the instruction card attached it is all ready for a friend. Take it to a summer cook-out as a hostess gift. To "pretty it up", print the recipe card on colored paper, add stickers or rubber stamping to the card. Make a matching "To-From" card. If you have fabric scraps, cut one and wrap it around the mix, tying it together with matching ribbons. Hot glue a silk flower or trinket to the bow. Easy to decorate this mix with any of your sewing, scrapbooking or crafting scraps.

Mix For Fruit Smoothies

1/2 cup powdered coffee creamer - unflavored or vanilla
scant 1/4 cup Jello® gelatin (measure so you get 2 mixes from one 4-serving package of gelatin.) Choose any flavor - see notes on Pg. 8.
1/4 cup powdered sugar

1. Mix all dry ingredients in a small bowl.
2. Place mix into a zipper sandwich bag.
3. Decorate if giving as a gift (see Pg. 5).
4. Attach instructions below. Write the name of your smoothie mix on the line on the card. (See Pg. 8 for ideas on naming your mix.)

_____

Make a blender full of Fruit Smoothies with this mix!

1. Place 2 cups milk (can use water, it is not as good) into a blender.
2. Add mix and blend briefly.
3. Add 2 cups crushed ice (or small cubes) and blend until smooth and creamy.
4. If desired, add a banana or 1 cup of fruit (like berries, sliced peaches, etc.) Works best if fruit is frozen. Can also add one 6-8 oz. carton yogurt or 1 cup ice cream, sherbet or frozen yogurt.

Makes approx. 3 1/2 cups (4 cups with fruit or ice cream).

Give This Fruit Smoothie Mix As A Gift
Read about this on pg. 5.

Keep Some Mixes On Hand For A Fast Smoothie

Make up some mixes for yourself. Attach the recipe card with the flavor written on it. Good for "Pick-Me-Up" on a hot summer day. Good to keep in the RV or at the lake house.

Mix For Sugar Free Fruit Smoothies

1/2 cup powdered coffee creamer- unflavored
1 1/2 tsp. sugar free Jello® gelatin (measure so you get 2 mixes from one 4-serving package of sugar free gelatin.) Choose any sugar free flavor - see notes on Pg. 8.
1/3 cup Splenda® sugar substitute

1. Mix all dry ingredients in a small bowl.
2. Place mix into a zipper sandwich bag.
3. Decorate if giving as a gift (see Pg. 5)
4. Attach instructions below. Write the name of your smoothie mix on the line on the card. (See Pg. 8 for ideas on naming your mix.) Be sure to include the words "Sugar-Free" in the name.

_____

Make a blender full of Sugar Free Fruit Smoothies with this mix!

1. Place 2 cups milk (can use water, it is not as good) into a blender.
2. Add mix and blend briefly.
3. Add 2 cups crushed ice (or small cubes) and blend until smooth and creamy.
4. If desired, add a banana or 1 cup of fruit (like berries, sliced peaches, etc.) Works best if fruit is frozen when added to smoothie.(It will then contain natural sugar from those fruits and won't be sugar free.)

Makes approx. 3 1/2 cups (4 cups with fruit).

Give This Fruit Smoothie Mix As A Gift
Read about this on pg. 5.

Keep Some Mixes On Hand For A Fast Smoothie
Read about this on pg. 6.

Choose Cappuccino Mix Flavors - (Recipe - Pg. 4)

General Foods Intl. Coffees® come in these flavors:
Cafe Francais, Cafe Vienna, Creme Caramel, French Vanilla Cafe, French Vanilla Nut, Hazelnut Belgian Cafe, Italian Cappuccino, Kahlua Cafe, Orange Cappuccino, Suisse Mocha, Swiss White Chocolate, Viennese Chocolate Cafe.

Any of these would make good cappuccino mixes. Also, other brands that are similar would work, too. To use another brand, start with 1/4 cup and make the mix. Then make the frozen cappuccino and see if you like it. Does it need more or less of the instant flavored coffee?

Powdered coffee creamer comes in these flavors:
Amaretto, Chocolate, Cinnamon Vanilla, French Vanilla, Hazelnut, Irish Creme, Vanilla Caramel, Vanilla Nut.

Try to imagine all the flavor combinations you can make by mix and matching these flavored coffees and coffee creamers!

Choose Fruit Smoothie Mix Flavors - (Recipe - Pg. 6)

Jello® brand gelatin comes in these flavors:
(The ones in bold type are the more popular flavors of smoothies and the ones I would recommend trying.)

Apricot, Berry Blue, Black Cherry, Cherry, Cranberry, Cranberry-Raspberry, Grape, **Pineapple**, Lemon, Lime, **Mango**, Mixed Fruit, Orange, **Peach**, **Raspberry**, **Strawberry**, **Strawberry-Banana**, Strawberry-Kiwi and Wild Strawberry, X-Treme Watermeon, X-Treme Wild Berry

Following are the Jello® sugar free flavors:
Black Cherry, Cherry, Cranberry, Lemon, Lime, Mandarin Orange, **Mixed Fruit**, Orange, **Peach**, **Raspberry**, **Strawberry**, **Strawberry-Banana**, Strawberry-Kiwi and **Wild Berry**.

Name Your Fruit Smoothie Mix - (Recipe - Pg. 6)

1. You need to identify the fruit flavor ("Peach Smoothie Mix").
2. Do you want to give it one of those "cute" smoothie names that you see at the Smoothie bars? Like "Peach Madness Smoothie Mix" or "Peach Paradise Smoothie Mix".
3. Do you want to name it after yourself, your family, the school team, the club? Those kind of names could be "Mary's Peach Smoothie Mix", "Smith's Cool Peach Smoothie Mix", "Battlin' Billies Peach Madness Smoothie Mix", "Red Hat Peach Paradise Smoothies Mix".

Raspberry Lime Smoothie

2/3 cup water
1/4 cup frozen limeade concentrate
2 cups frozen raspberries
1 banana, broken into quarters
1 cup lime sherbet or vanilla ice cream

1. Place ingredients into blender in order listed above.
2. Blend on high speed until thoroughly blended and creamy. (May have to stop blender and stir once or twice.)

Makes approx. 3 cups.

Strawberry Lime Smoothie

2/3 cup water
1/4 cup frozen limeade concentrate
2 cups frozen whole strawberries
1 banana, broken into quarters
1 cup strawberry ice cream or lime sherbet

1. Place ingredients into blender in order listed above.
2. Blend on high speed until thoroughly blended and creamy. (May have to stop blender and stir once or twice.)

Makes approx. 3 cups.

Blueberry Lemon Smoothie

2/3 cup water
1/4 cup frozen lemonade concentrate
2 cups frozen blueberries
1 banana, broken into quarters
1 cup lemon sorbet or vanilla ice cream

1. Place ingredients into blender in order listed above.
2. Blend on high speed until thoroughly blended and creamy. (May have to stop blender and stir once or twice.)

Makes approx. 3 cups.

Watermelon Smoothie

1 cup orange juice
1 cup milk
1 (6 oz. to 8 oz.) carton lemon yogurt
1 Tb. honey
1 1/2 cups seeded watermelon chunks
1 cup crushed ice (or small cubes)

1. Place ingredients into blender in order listed above.
2. Blend on high speed until thoroughly blended and creamy. (May have to stop blender and stir once or twice.)

Makes approx. 4 1/2 cups.

Watermelon Raspberry Smoothie

1 cup milk
2 cups seeded watermelon chunks
1 cup frozen raspberries
1 cup raspberry or swirl sherbet
1 cup crushed ice (or small cubes)

1. Place ingredients into blender in order listed above.
2. Blend on high speed until thoroughly blended and creamy. (May have to stop blender and stir once or twice.)

Makes approx. 4 cups.

Watermelon Shake

1 cup watermelon juice*
1/2 cup milk
3 cups vanilla ice cream or pineapple sherbet

1. Place ingredients into blender in order listed above.
2. Blend on high speed until thoroughly blended and creamy. (May have to stop blender and stir once or twice.)

Makes approx. 3 1/2 cups.

*Make juice by placing seeded watermelon cubes into a food processor. Process until smooth, then strain though a strainer, using your fingers to press out all the available juice. Use the juice and discard the pulp.

Strawberry Peach Smoothie

1 cup strawberry/banana nectar or white grape juice
3/4 cup frozen whole strawberries
1 1/4 cups frozen peach slices
1 banana, broken into quarters
2 Tb. honey
Optional: Add 1 cup flavored or plain yogurt or 1 cup ice cream, sherbet or frozen yogurt.

1. Place ingredients into blender in order listed above.
2. Blend on high speed until thoroughly blended and creamy. (Will have to stop blender and stir once or twice.)

Makes approx. 2 1/2 cups (3 cups with ice cream added).

Strawberry Banana Smoothie

1 cup strawberry/banana nectar or white grape juice
2 Tb. honey
1 cup frozen whole strawberries
2 small to medium bananas, broken in half
1 cup crushed ice (or small cubes)
Optional: Add 1 cup flavored or plain yogurt or 1 cup ice cream, sherbet or frozen yogurt. (Try with Banana Split Flavor Ice Cream!)

1. Place ingredients into blender in order listed above.
2. Blend on high speed until thoroughly blended and creamy. (May have to stop blender and stir once or twice.)

Makes approx. 3 cups (3 1/2 cups with ice cream added).

Fruit Smoothies

Pina Colada Smoothie

1 cup pineapple juice
1/2 cup canned cream of coconut (like Coco Lopez®)
1 banana, broken into quarters
2 cups crushed ice (or small cubes)

1. Place ingredients into blender in order listed above.
2. Blend on high speed until thoroughly blended and creamy. (May have to stop blender and stir once or twice.)

Makes approx. 3 1/2 cups.

Pina Colada Cream Smoothie

Add 6 oz to 8 oz. carton pina colada yogurt to recipe above.

Makes approx. 4 cups.

Rich Pina Colada Smoothie

Add 1 cup pineapple sherbet to recipe at top of page.
Makes approx. 4 cups.

Apricot Berry Smoothie

1 (11.5 oz.) can Kerns® (by Libby Foods®) apricot nectar
   (or 1 cup white grape juice)
1 (15 oz.) can apricot halves in heavy syrup, undrained
1 banana, broken into 4 pieces
2 cups crushed ice (or small cubes)

1 cup frozen whole strawberries or blackberries or
   raspberries

1. Place first 4 ingredients into blender in order listed above.
2. Blend on high speed until thoroughly blended and creamy. (May have to stop blender and stir once or twice.)
3. Add berries. Blend well.

Makes approx. 5 cups.

12   Fruit Smoothies

Honey and Milk Fruit Smoothies
Use any fruit you like - with milk instead of fruit juice.

1 cup milk
2 cups frozen fruit
1 banana, broken into quarters
2 Tb. honey
Optional: Add 1 cup flavored or plain yogurt, or any
　　flavor ice cream, frozen yogurt or sherbet.

1. Place ingredients into blender in order listed above.
2. Blend on high speed until thoroughly blended and
　　creamy. (May have to stop blender and stir once or twice.)

Makes approx. 3 cups (3 1/2 cups with ice cream).

Simple Yogurt Smoothies

　　Unlimited flavor choices - any juice flavor or
juice combo + any flavor yogurt.

1 cup any flavor juice or juice blend
1 cup (or a 6 oz. carton) any flavor yogurt*
　　*if using plain unflavored yogurt add 1 Tb. honey
1/2 crushed ice (or small cubes)
Optional: Add 1 cup frozen berries or frozen sliced fruit

1. Place ingredients into blender in order listed above.
2. Blend on high speed until thoroughly blended and
　　creamy. (May have to stop blender and stir once or twice.)

Makes approx. 2 1/2 cups without fruit or 3 cups with fruit.

Fruit Smoothies　　13

Fruit Smoothies - Basic Recipe

Follow the recipes on this page for ANY flavor fruit smoothie. Different flavors to try are on Pg. 15.

1 cup any flavor or blend of juice
2 cups frozen* fruit
1 banana, broken into quarters

1. Place ingredients into blender in order listed above.
2. Blend on high speed until thoroughly blended and creamy. (May have to stop blender and stir once or twice.)

*Buy frozen fruit in bags in the freezer case. Make smoothies with FROZEN FRUIT. This makes the smoothie cold with no need for ice.

Makes approx. 3 cups.

Cream Fruit Smoothies - Basic Recipe

Add a 6 oz to 8 oz. carton any flavor yogurt to Basic Fruit Smoothie recipe above. (Or use plain yogurt and 1 Tb. honey.)

Makes approx. 3 cups.

Rich Fruit Smoothie - Basic Recipe

Add 1 cup ice cream, frozen yogurt or sherbet to the recipe at the top of the page. Also good with only 1/2 cup ice cream.

Makes approx. 3 1/2 cups.

> See page 15 for flavor combinations to use with these basic recipes.

Fruit Smoothie Flavors For Basic Recipe

Use ingredients below with basic recipes on page 14.
Use exactly as written below or vary the fruit, juice, yogurt to make your own special combinations.
Or use what you have on hand - it may turn out to be your favorite flavor!

BLUEBERRY
white grape juice
frozen blueberries
banana
blueberry yogurt (opt.)
vanilla ice cream (opt.)

BLACKBERRY
white grape juice
frozen blackberries
banana
raspberry yogurt (opt.)
vanilla ice cream or lemon
    or pineapple sherbet

CHERRY
Libby's Juicy Juice® - Cherry
frozen dark sweet cherries
banana
cherry yogurt (opt.)
vanilla or cherry ice crm. (opt.)

RASPBERRY
any raspberry juice blend
frozen raspberries
banana
raspberry yogurt (opt.)
any sherbet or vanilla
    cream or frozen yog. (opt.)

MIXED BERRY
cran-raspberry juice
frozen mixed berries (in
    a freezer bag - rasp, blue,
    strawb. and blackberries)
banana
any berry flavor yogurt (opt.)
strawberry ice cream or
    swirl sherbet (opt.)

CRAN-RASPBERRY
cran-raspberry juice
frozen raspberries
banana
raspberry yogurt
swirl sherbet or van-
    illa ice cream (opt.)

Fruit Smoothies   15

Basic Fruit Smoothie Recipe - With Honey

Follow the recipes on this page for fruit smoothies with a little honey as a sweetener. These fruits need that extra sweetness. Different flavors to try are on Pg. 17.

1 cup any flavor or blend of juice
2 cups frozen fruit
1 banana, broken into quarters
2 Tb. honey

1. Place ingredients into blender in order listed above.
2. Blend on high speed until thoroughly blended and creamy. (May have to stop blender and stir once or twice.)

Makes approx. 3 cups.

Fruit Cream Smoothie With Honey - Basic Recipe

Add a 6 oz to 8 oz. carton any flavor yogurt to Fruit Smoothie recipe above.

Makes approx. 3 cups.

Rich Fruit Smoothie With Honey - Basic Recipe

Add 1 cup ice cream, frozen yogurt or sherbet to the recipe at the top of the page.

Makes approx. 3 1/2 cups.

See page 17 for flavor combinations to use with these basic recipes.

Fruit Smoothies

Fruit Smoothies With Honey - Flavors

Use ingredients below with recipes on Pg. 16.
Use these ingredients exactly as written below or vary the fruit, juice, yogurt to make your own special combinations. Or use what you have on hand - any combination will be good.

PEACH
peach nectar or OJ
frozen peach slices
banana
honey
peach yogurt (opt.)
peach ice cream (opt.)

PEACH/ORANGE
orange juice
frozen peach slices
banana
honey
peach yogurt (opt.)
orange sherbet (opt.)

STRAWBERRY
apple juice or strawberry
    nectar or strawberry blend
frozen whole strawberries
banana
honey
strawberry yogurt (opt.)
strawb. or vanilla ice cr. (opt.)

STRAWBERRY/GRAPEFRUIT
grapefruit juice
frozen whole strawberries
banana
honey
strawberry yogurt (opt.)
strawb. or vanilla ice cr.(opt.)

STRAWBERRY/ORANGE
orange juice
frozen whole strawberries
banana
honey
strawberry yogurt (opt.)
orange sherbet or straw-
    berry ice cream (opt.)

STRAWBERRY/PINEAPPLE
pineapple juice
frozen whole strawberries
banana
honey
strawberry yogurt (opt.)
pineapple sherbet or straw-
    berry ice cream (opt.)

MANGO
mango, peach or apricot
    nectar; or orange juice
frozen mango chunks
banana
honey
peach yogurt (opt.)
orange sherbet or vanilla
  ice cream (opt.)

PINEAPPLE/MANGO
pineapple juice
frozen mango chunks
banana
honey
pineapple yogurt (opt.)
pineapple sherbet (opt.)

Fruit Smoothies   17

Peanut Butter Smoothie

1 cup plain unflavored yogurt
1/2 cup creamy peanut butter
1 banana, broken into quarters
1/2 cup milk
1 Tb. honey
1 tsp. vanilla extract
1 cup crushed ice (or small cubes)

1. Place ingredients into blender in order listed above.
2. Blend on high speed until thoroughly blended and creamy. (May have to stop blender and stir once or twice.)

Makes approx. 2 1/2 cups.

Peanut Butter Milkshake

Add 1 cup vanilla ice cream (or frozen yogurt) to Peanut Butter Smoothie recipe above.

Makes approx. 3 cups.

Peanut Butter And Jelly Smoothie Or Milkshake

Add 1/4 cup grape or strawberry jelly to either recipe above. Taste and add 1 to 2 Tb. more jelly, if desired.

Chocolate Peanut Butter Smoothie Or Milkshake

Add 2 Tb. chocolate syrup to either the PB Smoothie or PB Milkshake recipes above.

Peanut Butter Banana Smoothie

Add 1 more banana and 1 more cup ice to Smoothie recipe at the top of the page.
Makes approx. 3 1/2 cups.

Eggnog Smoothie

2 cups prepared eggnog (in the dairy case at holiday time)
1 tsp. vanilla extract
1 tsp. nutmeg
1 banana, broken into quarters
2 cups ice

1. Place ingredients into blender in order listed above.
2. Blend on high speed until thoroughly blended and creamy. (May have to stop blender and stir once or twice.)

Makes approx. 4 cups.

Eggnog Shake

2 cups prepared eggnog (in the dairy case at holiday time)
2 tsp. vanilla extract
1 tsp. nutmeg
3 cups "homemade" vanilla flavor ice cream (or eggnog ice cream)

1. Place ingredients into blender in order listed above.
2. Blend on high speed until thoroughly blended and creamy. (May have to stop blender and stir once or twice.)

Makes approx. 4 cups.

Eggnog Shake Specialty Blender Cocktail
Add 1/3 cup rum, bourbon or brandy to above recipe.

Smoothies & Shakes   19

Pumpkin Smoothie

1/2 cup milk
1 cup canned pumpkin pie filling (not plain mashed pumpkin, but pumpkin pie filling)
2 cups ice
1 1/2 tsp. pumpkin pie spice (or blend nutmeg and cinnamon)
1 banana, broken into quarters

1. Place ingredients into blender in order listed above.
2. Blend on high speed until thoroughly blended and creamy. (May have to stop blender and stir once or twice.)

Makes approx. 3 1/2 cups.

Pumpkin Cream Smoothie

Add 1 cup plain unflavored yogurt and 1 Tb. honey to recipe above.

Makes approx. 3 1/2 cups.

Rich Pumpkin Smoothie

Add 1 cup vanilla ice cream or frozen yogurt to recipe at top of page.

Makes approx. 4 cups.

Smoothies & Shakes

Pumpkin Eggnog Smoothie

2 cups prepared eggnog (in the dairy case at holiday time)
1 tsp. vanilla extract
1 tsp. nutmeg
1 cup canned pumpkin pie filling (not plain mashed pumpkin, but pumpkin pie filling)
1 banana, broken into quarters
2 cups ice

1. Place ingredients into blender in order listed above.
2. Blend on high speed until thoroughly blended and creamy. (May have to stop blender and stir once or twice.)

Makes approx. 5 cups.

Pumpkin Eggnog Shake

2 cups prepared eggnog (in the dairy case at holiday time)
2 tsp. vanilla extract
1 tsp. nutmeg
1 cup canned pumpkin pie filling (not plain mashed pumpkin, but pumpkin pie filling).
3 cups "homemade" vanilla flavor ice cream (or eggnog ice cream)

1. Place ingredients into blender in order listed above.
2. Blend on high speed until thoroughly blended and creamy. (May have to stop blender and stir once or twice.)

Makes approx. 4 1/2 cups.

Pumpkin Eggnog Shake
Specialty Blender Cocktail

Add 1/3 cup rum or bourbon to above recipe.

Smoothies & Shakes

Juicy Sherbet Shake - Basic Recipe
(See some flavor ideas below.)

1 cup any flavor juice or juice blend or nectar
2 cups any flavor sherbet or sorbet
Optional: 1/2 cup any kind of berries or cut up fruit

1. Place ingredients into blender in order listed above.
2. Blend on high speed until thoroughly blended and creamy. (May have to stop blender and stir once or twice.)

Makes approx. 2 cups without fruit, 2 3/4 cups with fruit.

Juicy Sherbet Shake - Flavors
Use these flavor combinations with the recipe above.

Orange Juice and Orange Sherbet
Limeade and Lime Sherbet
Lemonade and Lemon Sorbet
Orange Juice and Swirl Sherbet
Pineapple Juice and Pineapple Sherbet
Cran-Raspberry Juice and Raspberry Sorbet
Use any can of "nectar*" with pineapple sherbet.

Mix and match any of the above flavors like orange juice with raspberry sorbet or pineapple juice with lime sherbet.

*Kerns Nectar® (by Libby® foods) come in these flavors:
Apple, Apricot, Apricot/Mango, Banana/Pineapple, Guava, Papaya, Strawberry, Peach, Pear, Pineapple/Coconut, Strawberry/Banana, Pineapple/Orange/Passion Fruit, Kiwi/Strawberry, Mango,

---
Juicy Sherbet Shakes
Specialty Blender Cocktails

Add 1/4 cup rum or vodka to the recipe at top of page.

Shakes

Ice Cream Shake - Basic Recipe

1 cup milk
2 tsp. vanilla extract
3 cups any flavor ice cream (or frozen yogurt)

1. Place ingredients into blender in order listed above.
2. Blend on high speed until thoroughly blended and creamy. (May have to stop blender and stir once or twice.)

Makes approx. 3 cups.

Ice Cream Frosties - Reese's PB® Cups

1/2 cup milk
1/2 cup chopped Reese's Peanut Butter Cups® candies
1/2 cup Reese's Pieces® candies
4 cups vanilla ice cream or frozen yogurt

1. Place ingredients into blender in order listed above.
2. Blend on high speed until thoroughly blended and creamy. (Will have to stop blender and stir several times.)

Makes approx. 4 cups.

Ice Cream Frosties - Oreos®/M&M's®

1/2 cup milk
1/2 cup crushed Oreo® cookies
1/2 cup M&M's® candies
4 cups vanilla ice cream or frozen yogurt

1. Place ingredients into blender in order listed above.
2. Blend on high speed until thoroughly blended and creamy. (Will have to stop blender and stir several times.)

Makes approx. 4 cups.

Make Your Own Flavors Ice Cream Frosties

Use any kind of cookie and candy you think will crush and blend well. Don't use hard candies - they will be too cold and hard to enjoy in the shake. Or blend two kinds of candies or two kinds of cookies. Use the recipe above for amounts. Use any flavor of ice cream you think would go well with the cookies and candies.

Shakes

Vanilla Or Chocolate Shake

1 cup milk
2 tsp. vanilla extract
3 cups vanilla ice cream (or frozen yogurt)
For Chocolate Shake add 1/4 cup chocolate syrup
    (this tastes better than using chocolate ice cream)

1. Place ingredients into blender in order listed above.
2. Blend on high speed until thoroughly blended and creamy. (May have to stop blender and stir once or twice.)

Makes approx. 3 cups.

Vanilla Or Chocolate Malt

1 cup milk
2 tsp. vanilla extract
1/4 cup Nestle Carnation® malted milk powder (sold on the hot chocolate mix aisle in the grocery store)
3 cups vanilla ice cream (or frozen yogurt)
For Chocolate Malt add 1/4 cup chocolate syrup
    (this tastes better than using chocolate ice cream)

1. Place ingredients into blender in order listed above.
2. Blend on high speed until thoroughly blended and creamy. (May have to stop blender and stir once or twice.)
3. Taste. Add 1 more Tb. malted milk powder if desired.

Makes approx. 3 cups.

Vanilla Or Chocolate Shake Or Malt With Oreos®

Add 6 Oreo® cookies to any recipe above. Break cookies in half before adding. Blend well.

Dulce de Leche Shake

1 (14 oz.) can sweetened condensed milk
1 cup milk
1/4 cup Smucker's® Dulce de Leche sauce or any
    caramel sauce (an ice cream topping)
1 tsp. vanilla
1/2 tsp. cinnamon
1 1/2 cups "homemade" vanilla ice cream
2 cups crushed ice (or small cubes)

1. Place ingredients into blender in order listed above.
2. Blend on high speed until thoroughly blended and
    creamy. (May have to stop blender and stir once or twice.)

Makes approx. 5 cups.

Mud Pie Shake

1 (14 oz.) can sweetened condensed milk
1 cup milk
2 Tb. chocolate syrup
1 tsp. vanilla
1 tsp. instant coffee powder
1 cup chocolate ice cream
2 cups crushed ice (or small cubes)

1. Place ingredients into blender in order listed above.
2. Blend on high speed until thoroughly blended and
    creamy. (May have to stop blender and stir once or twice.)

Makes approx. 4 cups.

Dulce de Leche Or Mud Pie Shake
Specialty Blender Cocktail

Add 1/3 cup rum to either recipe above.

Shakes   25

Banana Milkshake

1 cup milk
1 cup banana cream yogurt or plain yogurt
2 small to medium bananas, broken in half
1/4 tsp. nutmeg or pumpkin pie spice
1 tsp. vanilla
2 Tb. honey
2 cups crushed ice (or small ice cubes)

1. Place ingredients into blender in order listed above.
2. Blend on high speed until thoroughly blended and creamy. (May have to stop blender and stir once or twice

Makes approx. 4 cups.

Banana Split Milkshake

1 cup milk
1 (8 oz.) can crushed pineapple, undrained
1/4 cup chocolate syrup
1 tsp. vanilla
3/4 cup frozen whole strawberries
2 small to medium bananas, broken in half
2 cups vanilla ice cream

1. Place ingredients into blender in order listed above.
2. Blend on high speed until thoroughly blended and creamy. (May have to stop blender and stir once or twice.)

Makes approx. 5 cups.

Italian Cream "Cake" Milkshake

3/4 cup canned cream of coconut (like Coco Lopez®)
1 (8 oz.) block cream cheese, cut into 6 to 8 pieces
1/2 cup pecans
1 tsp. vanilla
1/2 cup milk
1 cup vanilla ice cream (or frozen yogurt)
2 cups crushed ice (or small cubes)

1. Place ingredients into blender in order listed above.
2. Blend on high speed until thoroughly blended and creamy. (Will have to stop blender and stir once or twice.)

Makes approx. 5 cups.

---

*Italian Cream "Cake" Milkshake
Specialty Blender Cocktail*
Add 1/3 cup rum to above recipe.

Bananas Foster Milkshake

1 (14 oz.) can sweetened condensed milk
1 cup milk
2 small to medium bananas
1/4 cup caramel sauce (an ice cream topping)
1 tsp. vanilla
1/2 tsp. cinnamon
1 1/2 cups "homemade" vanilla ice cream
2 cups crushed ice (or small cubes)

1. Place ingredients into blender in order listed above.
2. Blend on high speed until thoroughly blended and creamy. (May have to stop blender and stir once or twice.)

Makes approx. 5 cups.

---

*Bananas Foster Milkshake
Specialty Blender Cocktail*
Add 1/3 cup rum to above recipe.

Shakes

Caramel Apple Milkshake

1 cup apple juice
1/3 cup caramel sauce (an ice cream topping)
1 tsp. vanilla extract
1/2 tsp. cinnamon
2 cups vanilla ice cream (or frozen yogurt)
2 cups crushed ice (or small cubes)

1. Place ingredients into blender in order listed above.
2. Blend on high speed until thoroughly blended and creamy. (May have to stop blender and stir once or twice.)

Makes approx. 3 1/2 cups.

Purple Cow Shake

1 cup grape juice
1 Tb. lemon juice
2 tsp. vanilla
3 cups vanilla ice cream

1. Place ingredients into blender in order listed above.
2. Blend on high speed until thoroughly blended and creamy. (May have to stop blender and stir once or twice.)

Makes approx. 3 1/2 cups.

Milk Punch Specialty Blender Cocktail

1/2 cup milk
1 Tb. rum
1 Tb. bourbon
2 cups "homemade" vanilla ice cream (or frozen yogurt)
1/2 cup crushed ice (or small cubes)

1. Place ingredients into blender in order listed above.
2. Blend on high speed until thoroughly blended and creamy. (May have to stop blender and stir several times.)

Makes approx. 2 cups.

Peppermint Shake

1 cup milk
2 tsp. vanilla extract
3 cups vanilla ice cream (or frozen yogurt) (or use peppermint ice cream and only 10 candies)
20 small round peppermint candy disks, unwrapped (use either red or green peppermints, don't mix them)

several small (2" to 3") candy canes for garnish (opt.)

1. Place ingredients into blender (except candy canes) in order listed above.
2. Blend on high speed until thoroughly blended and creamy. (May have to stop blender and stir once or twice.)

Makes approx. 3 1/2 cups.

Peppermint Shake
Specialty Blender Cocktail

Add 1/3 cup white Creme de Menthe liqueur to above recipe. (Can add green Creme de Menthe if that is what you have on hand. It will turn the pink milkshake pale green, but the color looks good.) Or add 1/3 cup Peppermint Schnapps Liqueur.

Coconut Shake

3/4 cup canned cream of coconut (like Coco Lopez*)
1 cup milk
1 1/2 cups vanilla ice cream or frozen yogurt
1 cup ice
Optional: sprinkle individual servings with flaked coconut

1. Place ingredients into blender in order listed above.
2. Blend on high speed until thoroughly blended and creamy. (May have to stop blender and stir once or twice.)

Makes approx. 3 cups.

Coconut Shake Specialty Blender Cocktail
Add 1/3 rum to above recipe.

Shakes

Cappuccino Shake

1 cup strong brewed coffee (room temp. or cold)
1 tsp. vanilla
3 cups coffee ice cream

1. Place ingredients into blender in order listed above.
2. Blend on high speed until thoroughly blended and creamy. (May have to stop blender and stir once or twice.)
3. Garnish each serving with a squirt of squirt whipped cream and a sprinkle of cinnamon, if desired.

Makes approx. 3 cups.

Mocha Cappuccino Shake

Add 2 Tb. Nesquik® chocolate drink mix to recipe above. Garnish with squirt whipped cream and chocolate sprinkles.

Cappuccino or Mocha Cappuccino Shake Specialty Blender Cocktail
Add 1/3 cup Kahlua or rum to either shake recipe above.

Frozen Cappuccino or Sugar Free Frozen Cappuccino

See recipes on Pgs. 4-5. These are recipes for mixes but can be made right in your blender without the step of making the mix. They are great tasting and easy.

Liqueur Milkshake Specialty Blender Cocktail*
(*Like Kahlua, Amaretto, Chambord, Grand Marnier)

2 cups vanilla ice cream (or frozen yogurt)
1/3 cup liqueur (can use the least expensive brand)
1 cup crushed ice (or small cubes)

1. Place ingredients into blender in order listed above.
2. Blend on high speed until thoroughly blended and creamy. (May have to stop blender and stir once or twice.)

Makes approx. 3 1/2 cups.

Chai Tea Latté Smoothie

1/2 cup milk
1/2 cup + 1 Tb. Chai tea concentrate (sold in health food stores - refrigerated in cartons - Oregon® and Tazo® are two brands.)
1 1/2 Tb. honey
1 tsp. vanilla
1 banana, broken into quarters
2 cups ice

1. Place ingredients into blender in order listed above.
2. Blend on high speed until thoroughly blended and creamy. (May have to stop blender and stir once or twice.)
3. Taste and add 1 Tb. more Chai tea concentrate if desired.

Makes approx. 3 cups.

Chai Tea Latté Cream Smoothie

Add 1 cup plain unflavored yogurt and 1 Tb. more honey to recipe above.

Makes approx. 3 1/2 cups.

Rich Chai Tea Latté Smoothie

Add 1 cup "homemade" vanilla ice cream to recipe at top of page.

Makes approx. 3 1/2 cups.

Chai

Milk Shakers Spoonful Mix

This is from the book "Special Spoonfuls" (see copyright page for ordering information). This is a simple "little giftie" of a mix to flavor milk. It is fun for kids.

1 Tb. + 1 tsp. instant pudding mix* (not sugar free)
plastic wrap and an ordinary plastic spoon (can be a color or white)

*Choose one of these instant pudding flavors: Vanilla, White Chocolate, Lemon, Butterscotch, Banana Cream, Cheesecake.

1. Wrap pudding mix in a 6" square of plastic wrap (it will look like a little strawberry in size and shape.) Attach to spoon with scotch tape.
2. Cover mix with a piece of tissue paper, cellophane, decorative paper napkin or fabric scrap - and tie with a small ribbon.
3. Attach instructions below. Name it for whichever flavor you are using.

"Banana" Milk Shaker

1. Remove decorative wrapping from spoon, leaving mix inside plastic wrap and still attached to spoon.
2. Place one cup milk into a small plastic container with lid.
3. Hold spoon over milk. Cut open bag of mix so mix falls into milk.
4. Put lid on container and shake 30 seconds. Drink immediately.

Index

Amaretto Milkshake Cocktail	30	Mango Smoothie	17
Apricot Berry Smoothie	12	Milk Punch Cocktail	28
Banana Milkshake, Banana Split Milkshake	26	Mix - Frozen Cappuccino	4
Banana Strawberry Smoothie	11	Mix - Fruit Smoothies	6
Bananas Foster Milkshake or Cocktail	27	Mix - Sugar Free Frozen Cappuccino	5
Berry Apricot Smoothie	12	Mix - Sugar Free Fruit Smoothies	7
Blackberry Smoothie	15	Mixed Berry Smoothie	15
Blueberry Lemon Smoothie	9	Mixes	4 - 8
Blueberry Smoothie	15	Mocha Cappuccino Shake or Cocktail	30
Cappuccino Shake or Cocktail	30	Mud Pie Blender Shake or Cocktail	25
Caramel Apple Milkshake	28	Peach Orange Smoothie	17
Chai Tea Latté Smoothie	31	Peach Smoothie	17
Chambord Milkshake Cocktail	30	Peach Strawberry Smoothie	11
Cherry Smoothie	15	Peanut Butter Banana Smoothie	18
Chocolate Malt, or with Oreos added	24	Peanut Butter Smoothie or Milkshake	18
Chocolate PB Smoothie	18	Peanut Butter/Jelly Smoothie	18
Chocolate Shake, or with Oreos added	24	Peppermint Shake or Cocktail	29
Cocktails	19,21,22,25,27 29,30	Pina Colada Smoothie	12
Coconut Shake or Cocktail	29	Pumpkin Eggnog Cocktail	21
Cran-Raspberry Smoothie	15	Pumpkin Eggnog Smoothie or Shake	21
Dulce de Leche Shake or Cocktail	25	Pumpkin Smoothie	20
Eggnog Shake or Cocktail	19	Purple Cow Shake	28
Frozen Cappuccino - Mix	4	Raspberry Lime Smoothie	9
Fruit Smoothie - Basic Recipe	14-15	Raspberry Smoothie	15
Fruit Smoothie -Basic - With Honey	16-17	Raspberry Watermelon Smoothie	10
Fruit Smoothies Mix	6	Simple Yogurt Smoothies	13
Fruit Smoothies	9 -17	Strawberry Banana Smoothie	11
Grand Marnier Cocktail	30	Strawberry Grapefruit Smoothie	17
Honey And Milk Fruit Smoothie	13	Strawberry Lime Smoothie	9
Ice Cream Frosties - Oreos or Peanut Butter	23	Strawberry Orange Smoothie	17
Ice Cream Shake - Basic Recipe	23	Strawberry Peach Smoothie	11
Italian Cream "Cake" Shake or Cocktail	27	Strawberry Pineapple Smoothie	17
Juicy Sherbet Blender Shake or Cocktail	22	Strawberry Smoothie	17
Kahlua Milkshake Cocktail	30	Sugar Free Frozen Cappuccino Mix	5
Lemon Blueberry Smoothie	9	Sugar Free Fruit Smoothie Mix	7
Lime Raspberry Smoothie	9	Vanilla Malt or Shake, with Oreos added	24
Lime Strawberry Smoothie	9	Watermelon Raspberry Smoothie	10
Liqueur Blender Cocktails	30	Watermelon Shake or Smoothie	10
		Yogurt Smoothies	13